Rebel With A Cause

A MEMOIR

Published and Distributed by:
Professional Publishing House

Cover Design: Richard Ike

Formatting: Professional Publishing House

First Printing, August, 2010
10987654321

ISBN: 978-982-6704-4-6

Professional Publishing House
1425 W. Manchester, Suite B
Los Angeles, California 90047
(323) 750-3592
www.professionalpublishinghouse.com
E-mail: Drrosie@aol.com

Rebel With A Cause

A MEMOIR

Bill Jones

About The Author

Willie Jones A.K.A.—Bill Jones is the former owner of one of the most famous, prestigious private clubs in Los Angeles, B J's Gentlemen Club. Bill operated four clubs in Los Angeles. The film "Heat" was partly filmed at his club, starring Robert De Niro , Al Pacino and Tone Loc.

B. J. laid claim to being the best crap shooter on the West Coast. Crap shooters came from far away as New York, Saint Louis, Detroit and Tennessee to challenge B. J. However, they all returned home with empty pockets.

Table of Contents

Introduction

I was born in Kansas City, Missouri in a small wooded area called Leeds. Leeds was located about halfway between Kansas City, Missouri and Independence, Missouri. Leeds was divided into two parts; Allen's Additions and Couches Additions.

In Allen Addition, the streets were paved. In the Couches Addition where I lived, nothing was paved. The side where everyone lived had dirt roads. Everyone had wood burning stoves for cooking and heat. We had no electricity; we used coal oil lamps, for lighting the house. We had outside toilets and big tin tubs to bathe in. We bathed once a week on Saturday. Since I had three sisters, they all bathed before me. After each one finished, my mother would add a tea kettle full of hot water. By the time it was my turn, the water looked like soup!

The bathrooms at the grade school I went to were outside. The people living in Kansas City city limits didn't live in such primitive conditions. They all had inside facilities.

When I was old enough, I asked, "Mother, whose idea was it to live out in the woods?"

"It a long story," she replied, "and I will tell you when the time is right."

I was about sixteen then and the time didn't get right until just before my eighteenth birthday. We were on a fishing trip sitting side by side on a log; no one else was fishing near enough to hear what we were talking about. "Brother, I am going to tell you what you asked about a couple of years ago," she said. She went on say, "Everybody in Leeds was originally put there by Harriet Tubman's Underground Railroad as they were all wanted criminals in most of the Southern states."

"Does that include Grandpa?" I asked.

"Especially your grandpa, my father," she said. "You were named after your grandpa. He didn't like your father and was mostly responsible for him leaving town. His pet name for your father was lazy, good-for-nothing bastard. When you were born, your grandpa said he was going to raise you to be just like him; strong, hardworking and afraid of nothing."

My mother said that she was afraid for me because she knew of Grandpa's other characteristics. He was mean, violent, vengeful, and extremely destructive, if someone crossed him. My mother told me when he was mad at someone, he would drink two or three jars of his homemade wine and start talking to himself about what he intended to do to whoever he was mad at. She said that he had a special little plan he would mutter to himself. He would say that he was going to break his victim's back bone, paralyze his ribs, kill his kidneys and dare his heart to beat. Mom said he would mumble this over and over again.

I remember, one day I came home with a black eye. Grandpa asked me, "What happened, Lil Bubba?"

"I had a fight with a boy that was bigger than me," I told him, "and I was winning until the boy grabbed my hair and I was tender headed. So the boy threw me down and hit me in the eye."

Grandpa got mad as hell and this is what he said: "Goddamn, you little dumb bastard! You didn't have sense enough to grab his balls when he grabbed your hair?" He continued, "That boy is bigger than you, however, when you get to school tomorrow, you fight him again, but this time you do these things: Number one, you pick when the fight starts, number two, you pick where the fight starts, number three, you know he doesn't fight fair so you cheat first. When you see him, you walk right up to him and kick him in his nuts as hard as you can.

"This way you have the element of surprise and you picked the place to fight so stash a big stick close by. That first move should take all the fight out of the bastard. So black both his eyes and come on home. You won't have any more trouble out of him."

I learned a lot that day, and those lessons helped me all through life. Another thing he taught me was to never start trouble, but, by any means possible, end it. I had very little trouble after that in Leeds but after the seventh grade, you had to go to high school in Kansas City.

The city only had two schools for blacks. The house we lived in was next to the last house on top of a hill on an unpaved road. No sidewalk, so on a rainy day, you walked five blocks down this muddy road to where the street car turned around to go back to town. Your shoes, socks and the bottom of your pants would be muddy as hell when you got to school.

chapter one

My last name was Jones, so they started calling me Farmer Jones. One day, Grandpa asked me, "How you like school in the city?"

"It's okay," I replied, "except they tease me about all the mud and call me Farmer Jones."

Grandpa, looking me eyeball to eyeball, said, "Well, Little Bubba, you have to make an example out of those assholes."

"The main boy was a big tall fat guy," I said.

"Well, you make the example out of that one," Grandpa replied.

In the winter my sisters wore cotton stockings that came up to their knees. Grandpa taught me how to use my sister's stockings and win the

fight. Grandpa told me to get one of those stockings and put a rock about the size of an orange in it and tie a knot at the top of the stocking so it won't slip from your hand. When I got the chance, I should bash the fat boy in the head with it. Grandpa said if that didn't knock him out with the first blow, start running and he will chase you. He said run until his fat ass is out of breath and then stop and beat his big ass some more. "And I bet you nobody will call you Farmer Jones anymore," Grandpa added.

I did just that and Grandpa was right. That is when I made my mind up to rebel against anybody or anything that mistreated me. I had no more trouble.

Even though I had no more trouble with my peers, there would be many battles I had to fight as a result of meeting and falling in love with a white woman.

I completed high school in Michigan. In Michigan the schools were integrated and there were interracial relationships. I returned to Leeds, Missouri after completing high school. In Leeds, the schools, movies, etc were segregated. I was the first Black man in Missouri to date a white woman. I was eighteen and my girlfriend was twenty-six.

The police in Kansas City were determined to make an example of me. They tried to clean up their unsolved crimes by trying to attach them to me. By any means necessary—they wanted me off the streets and out of their town. They wanted to send a message that this was the first and the last and that there would be no more Blacks dating white woman in Kansas City. They wanted Black men to see what would happen to a Black man who crossed the colored line.

As the pages turn, you will see the many attempts made to have me taken away from the free world. Little did they know, my grandpa had turned me into being a rebel when there was a cause. So they had the wrong person to make an example out of.

Stories about me dominated the Kansas City newspapers and television stations for months. Yes, the police department was hell-bent on clearing the old crime book via accusing me of those unsolved crimes.

Most of the Blacks in Leeds were dumped there by the way of the Underground Railroad; this was an undeveloped woody area. Many of the Blacks were afraid to apply for a social security card, they were afraid of being caught. Therefore, many Blacks became entrepreneurs—hauling trash and dump for white people. My grandpa had a trash truck. He could not drive so he hired a driver. As the driver drove through town, he and my grandpa would ride in the truck cab. Meantime, I would be riding in the truck bed. We were all yelling out, "Trash man, trash man!"

Each trash man had his own trash route and every person respected the other man's route.

chapter two

I Met My
First Love--
She Was White

I turned eighteen in 1953 and met my first love at a ball game. There was only one problem--she was white. I was unaware that it was a problem until later on when it became a big problem. She was a very pretty girl. She wore a size 5/6 dress with long pretty black hair down to her waist. She had a sweet personality and a smile that made you feel good all over. I was so completely absorbed with this girl that I forgot that we were in a state where blacks couldn't go to the same schools, eat at the same restaurants or, even sit together in the same movie theaters. In short, the times were really segregated and racist.

Love can truly blind you to reality. Lola worked during the week but would come to my house every Friday after work and we would spend most of the weekends together. Lola would bring me a one hundred bill every Friday. Before then, I had never seen a one hundred dollar bill in my life. It wasn't just the money that made me love Lola, but, at the same time, I wasn't about to let her or the money go because white folks did not want me to be with her.

About six or seven weeks into our relationship on a Friday night my mom asked me to go to Gate's Bar-B-Que and get bar-b-que for everybody. "Good idea," I replied.

Lola said, "I'll ride with you," and I agreed.

Being with Lola seemed to occupy every feeling and thought that I was capable of having. We passed a black and white police car parked about two blocks from the Bar-B-Que place and I remembered that there was always one parked there when the place was open. They must've noticed Lola in the car because as we turned into the parking lot, they were right on us. The officer on the passenger side had his spot light on Lola. When he was positive that she was white, he got out of the car. His anger was obvious. It was exhibited in his sharp movements. He came to my side of the car, opened the door and snarled in a very mean voice, "Git out of the car, boy!" He sounded out of breath. His face was real red and he looked like what you would expect to see if you snatched the hood off of a Klansmen.

The other officer was still in the car on the radio so I knew there would be others there shortly. In no time there were at least seven to ten cars there as if they had cornered Public Enemy No.1. I never had trouble with the police before, so this was my first encounter with them and they took me to jail. I asked the officer, "What am I being arrested for?"

The officer retorted with anger in his voice, "For Suspicion."

"Suspicion of what?" I asked.

"Suspicion of burglary, robbery and rape."

It was then that I realized how serious these people were about segregation. I know that Kansas City, Kansas was one of the first to integrate, but Kansas City,

Missouri, was one of the last and they are only separated by a river. The racial issue had never bothered me before, but all of a sudden, it exploded right here in front of my face. I was born into segregation and expected it. In fact, I had never given any serious thought to it. Had I had a clue that I would meet and fall in love with Lola, I would have, without a doubt, given it every consideration.

I had never been to jail before so I had no idea what was going to happen next; it didn't take long to find out though. When I got there, they fingerprinted me and put me in a big room that had iron bunk beds with no mattresses, blankets or pillows. There were little holes about the size of a quarter all over the bottom of the steel bed and told me I would be there for three days and nights. What they didn't tell me was that every time there was a shift change for the detective, the jailer would come get me, handcuff me and take me to a small room where two detectives would come and question me.

All the questions were about Lola, not burglary, robbery or rape. It didn't take long to realize that they just wanted to get a look at the nigger that had the nerve to date a pretty white girl. The amount of hatred they had for me was unreal. Some of them would slap me out of the chair when I refused to answer the questions about sex with Lola. That was the longest 72 hours of my life. Most of them threatened my life if I kept seeing Lola, but they finally let me go.

Although we didn't go out in public together, we kept seeing and loving each other. Lola told me that when they took me to jail, they drove her home and told her, "If you keep seeing that nigger, you are going to get him killed." I must admit I was starting to become a little afraid now. I had seen the hatred in their eyes.

Lola and I changed our meeting place and time around. I started hanging out with my friends in Leeds on the weekends. We thought this would make the racist bastards think we had stopped seeing each other. I even left my car at home and rode with one of my friends most of the time, as they knew my car very well.

chapter three

I Was Innocent

It was during this time when six of us went to a party one weekend in one of the guy's new car. We hooked up with three girls at the party that lived in Kansas City, Kansas and promised to give them a ride back after the party. I wondered how we would fit nine people in a two-door Mercury, but we did. I had been drinking wine on an empty stomach, so when we started back, I passed out. I don't even remember when we dropped the girls off.

I was still passed out when these other idiots got back to Missouri and decided to rob a service station. How stupid was that? My friend Rick and one other fool left the rest of us parked about

a block and a half away and went back to rob the place. The attendant saw them coming and came outside to meet them. Rick told him it was a stick up. the man turned to run back and Rick tried to stop him by shooting him. He aimed for his leg, but the bullet went high, hitting his rib bone and ricochet into the back of his heart killing him instantly.

Rick and the other fool started running back toward the car. Rick was kind of fat, so he couldn't run as fast as the other fool. Ron's yelling and screaming woke me up. "Rick shot the man, Rick shot the man."

"Where is Rick?" I asked.

"He said he was coming!"

I looked out of the rear window and saw Rick staggering, huffing and puffing, out of breath, trying to make it to the car. The driver panicked and drove off. "Wait for Rick," I shouted, but he kept going.

I picked up a coke bottle from the floor and hit him in the head. As heavy as coke bottles were in those days, it broke. I was mad as hell! I told the driver to take me home.

When we got there we all got out and went in. The phone was ringing. It was Rick and he was crying and could hardly talk. "Come get me, cuz. Please come get me."

He told me the corner he was on. It was a vacant lot with a school bus, with a pay phone. My other friend and me went to get him.

Once I pick him up and took him back to my house, I took the gun from him, drove alone to Troost Lake and threw it in. When I got back home, I told the dumb asses to get out of my house, go home and keep their mouths shut. After that, I started staying home at night and having Lola come over.

In the meantime, one of the other fools, who was in the car the night of the shooting, decided to relieve his conscience by telling his uncle, who had a friend that worked at the county jail. One at a time, they went to each of the fools' house and arrested them. All the others were in jail before they came to arrest me.

When they arrested the others, they knocked on the door and announced

themselves. But when they came to get me, they didn't come to arrest me. They came to kill me. You see, they didn't knock on the door. Instead, they picked the lock on the back door and seven of them came in.

There were twin beds in my room and my buddy was there in one of them with one of Lola's friends. One cop turned on the light while the others snatched the cover off both beds at the same time. The other cops had their weapons cocked and aimed at me. It had nothing to do with the shooting at the gas station as my friends had already told them I was passed out and had no knowledge of their intention to rob the station. So they came to keep their promise to kill me and would have if those two white girls had not been there. By the way, we were all nude, and for the next month or more, all the news on TV was about us.

They were trying to clean the books; they were trying to attribute all the unsolved crimes to us. The TV had already made me the leader of a gang. Maybe because I went back to get my friend, maybe because I disposed of the murder weapon, but I think mostly to put me away forever for breaking their racial barrier.

The racial hatred they had for me caused them to over charge me. They got seven racist hillbillies to pick from the TV newscast and they said that I had robbed them. When I got to the county jail, they had filed eight charges against me. Seven were first-degree armed robbery with positive identification and one first degree premeditated murder charge. I was only guilty of accessory after the fact. All of the robbery victims were coerced to lie after they found out about Lola. She made several attempts to visit me but was turned away each time.

My mother came to visit me and told me Lola had given ten thousand dollars to an attorney who tried lots of murder cases and had won them all. His name was John C. Poulman.

What Lola didn't know was that Poulman was racist also. Three months passed and not once did Poulman come to see me. Finally, during the next month, he came to see me, along with a meek-

looking little man from Time Magazine, who had promised to pay my mother thirty-five thousand dollars for my life story.

I chose to see Poulman first. He was a big tall (6'3" or so,) well-dressed man who wore glasses. He also had a phony smile. Before he had a chance to say anything, I blurted out, "What took you so long to get here?"

He started turning red and clearing his throat. I could tell he was about to tell me a lie. He said he didn't want to see me until he had good news for me. He said he had been begging the prosecuting attorney to give me a break. He said he made so many trips that he got tired of him pestering him and he finally gave in. He put his hand on my shoulder. "My boy, you're gonna love me for this. I got him to agree to let you plead to a lesser charge and receive a twenty year sentence and I will personally promise to have you out in eight years!"

I was so insulted that this ass hole would be little my intelligence to that extent. As I got up from the desk, I said, "Are you out of your chicken shit mind?I was the only innocent one in the damn car. I had no idea those fools would try and rob that place, you stupid bastard."

He started to rise from his desk as he said, "You ungrateful nigger."

At the end of that word, I hit him right in the center of his glasses with a devastating right hand. The blow knocked him back against the wall where his head hit so hard, it stunned him. Blood was streaming down his face from the broken glasses. As he slid down to the floor, his legs were spread apart so I accepted the invitation to kick him in his family jewels a few times. After all, how much more trouble could I get into? The big punk was holding his face with his hands and screaming like a bitch.

I turned around just in time to see the little man from Time Magazine running like hell toward the elevator. I thought to myself how Grandpa would have been proud of me for the ass kicking I put on that big prejudiced bastard.

Well, after he got out of the hospital, there was no way he was coming back near me. However, he didn't want to return the ten thousand dollars, so he sent a young 26-yr-old Italian named Arnold Hill. He had just passed the bar

and was assigned to Poulman's office for six months until he could open his own practice. Arnold Hill and I were about the same size. He said that he wanted to see the guy who did that to Poulman. He told me Poulman had treated him like a flunky and he got exactly what he deserved. I knew then that I liked him.

He went on to say he had read the transcripts and that it was obvious the police were using my relationship with Lola to entice the so- called robbery victims to identify me as their robber. He told me a lot of his friends advised him not to defend me to avoid starting his career off with a loss. He defended his actions saying, but look what it would do for his career if he won a so-called impossible case.

"Mr. Jones," he said, "I like you and I think we can win this case."

Needless to say, I liked him too. He indicated he was working on an idea to use their ruthlessness against them. We shook hands and he told me he would be back in a week or ten days to explain his plan.

Like he promised, he was back in a week. He showed me a letter that he drafted that he was going to present to each of the alleged robbery victims. In essence, it stated it would eliminate a lot of red tape, if they would drop the robbery charge and the state would sentence me to the gas chamber with no problem. He explained that if we didn't dispose of all seven of the robbery charges, even if I got off the murder charge, they could give me twenty-five to thirty years on any one of those robbery charges. He said since they were lying anyway, it shouldn't be too hard to convince them to comply, thinking I would get the gas chamber as punishment. It would satisfy their resentment of me for dating Lola.

The plan worked and in a month, all the fraudulent robbery charges had been dropped. Mr. Hill said that the two guys who went to the station had pled guilty and to avoid the gas chamber, received life sentences.

"Now, Mr. Jones," Mr. Hill said, "we prepare for the murder charge.'

I asked him if he had anymore genius plans like the other one.

He smiled. "Not yet, but by court time I will!"

I had come to like and respect this man. For the first time since this madness began, I was beginning to believe that with God and Mr. Hill on my side, I had a chance. That was quite a bit to pray for and that is exactly what I prayed for, A LOT!

The head prosecutor for the state of Missouri was going to prosecute the case and when it came to murder, he had never lost a case. My attorney had never tried a case. The prosecutor, J. Donald O'Hern, was a small man, bald on the top with hair over his ears. The top of his head and face were blood red, as if he was angry and about to strike out at someone.

The judge instructed the jury that there could be only one of three outcomes; natural life with no chance of parole, the gas chamber or acquittal. Mr. Hill said his plan was to put me on the stand and all I had to do was tell the truth. He told me the prosecutor would try every way to make it look as if I had been awake and had knowledge of the plans to rob the station. They kept me on the stand for five long days. True enough, O'Hern used every tactic he could think of, but I was telling the truth and the truth speaks for itself.

Finally, O'Hern said he had no more questions and the court room was silent for a few seconds. Then the side door opened drawing everyone's attention to it and in walked the guy that snitched to his uncle and with him were the two detectives that manipulated the phony robbery charges. Mr. Hill put his hands on my shoulder and whispered to me they are trying to make him say you had knowledge. That is the only long shot they have left. The whole court room had their attention.

The guy slowly started turning his head from left to right indicating "No".

"Good," Mr. Hill said. "He didn't go for it!" After Mr. Hill rested his case, it was time for closing arguments. O'Hern was up first; the one thing I remember most was when he told the jury, "If you put this man back on the street, then put my family and me in the penitentiary where we will be safe." After Mr. Hill finished his closing argument it was turned over to the jury.

They took me to a different floor while we waited for the jury to deliberate. After about two hours, I was returned to the court room. The jury had reached a verdict. The judge asked the jury foreman, what the verdict was and he said, "Not Guilty!"

My mother ran from the back, yelling, "Thank you, Jesus, thank you, Jesus!" With tears streaming down her face, she threw her arms around Mr. Hill.

Mr. Hill was crying and me? Well, I was crying, and so weak in the knees that I was in shock. Never in my life had I had so much heartfelt admiration for a person as I felt at that time for Mr. Hill. He saved my life! Why did my life need to be saved? Simply because my biggest crime was I had fallen in love with Lola.

The greater white majority felt that, for a black man to fall in love with a white woman, it was a crime punishable by death. At least that is the way law enforcement felt and they had proven that to me.

I knew they had taken orders from higher-up racists and often wondered if it was the Ku Klux Klan. Anyway, back at the court room, when O'Hern heard the verdict, he turned really red, started coughing and clutching his chest. He staggered around and sat in a chair. He was bent over; I thought he was praying. At that time, we left so I could get released and go home.

The next day someone called my mother and told her that O'Hern had died. The next week, we got the news that Mr. Hill had been given the job of head prosecutor for the state of Missouri. I knew then what he meant when he said to his friends. Look what winning the impossible case would do for his political career. What a smart man! It brings to mind what my grandpa told me. "Lil Bubba, if you fail to plan, then you plan to fail." I feel blessed to have had two smart men in my life. Grandpa would be considered to be tougher and meaner than he was smart.

chapter four

The Police Wanted Me At Any Cost

My mother reminded me that the hatred the police had for me before was nothing compared to what it was going to be if I was released. She suggested that I leave town for a while upon my release. I told her not a chance. I knew the police had questioned each one of those guys before they came to arrest me, and they knew I was asleep when they decided to do that stupid shit. They knew I was guilty of accessory after the fact, but because of Lola, they tried to frame me for robbery and murder. For most of the time that I was in county jail, I thought they would be successful, so I mentally prepared myself to spend the rest of my life in prison.

While I was in the county jail, I was placed in the murder tank with the rest of the prisoners with the same charges and most of them were ex-convicts. This was my first time being arrested. I was only 5'7" with curly hair and told that I would have a tough time in the pen because they would never stop trying to make a punk out of me. Because of my grandpa, I knew I would rebel and kill whoever tried to do that to me, so I would probably never get out. No, I was not leaving town; they had me hard, tough and unafraid. I thought to myself, this is how Grandpa wanted me to be.

While in jail, a guy taught me the art of shooting crooked dice, loaded dice to be exact, and told me where to get them made in Kansas City, Kansas and who to ask for.

So, I started hanging out in night clubs, waiting on someone who had a little too much to drink and easy to get where we could win all of his money with the crooked dice. After a while, I discovered that having a pretty girl with me made it easier to lead them to the gambling place. This made it possible for me to sell more whisky; now I became a gambler and a bootlegger.

The pretty girl, who was my hustling partner, began to like me a lot, simply because when I won, I would cut her in a nice portion of the winnings. She would also sell the whisky while I gambled, so I gave her a cut of that as well. We were doing very well, but we noticed that we were being followed when we moved from place to place. I had been back on the street for about six months and had expected to be harassed before then, but the cop that was following us never lit us up or pulled us over. He stayed two car lengths behind us.

At that time, the penalty for carrying a firearm in Kansas City, Missouri was a fifty dollar fine or ten days on a Leeds farm. So, I always carried a gun. Had I not, I would have been the only person who didn't. So when we would see the police car following us, my girl Nikki, yes

I said my girl, would put the gun in her purse. To put it mildly, we had become very fond of one another. I thought if the police saw that I was interested in someone else, particularly a black girl, they would leave me alone.

When Nikki and I couldn't find anyone to break during the week, we would go to my friend's all night restaurant for breakfast. The policeman who followed us started coming in there too. He was a nice, easy-going older gentleman with a nice personality. Never once did he harass or approach us.

Nikki suggested we invite him to eat with us. Maybe then we could get to know him and find out why he is following us. I told her I was game.

One Monday as he sat at his regular counter seat, Nikki went up to him and invited him to our table. Much to my surprise he came over and joined us. He told us his name was Jack Cutter and his retirement was six months away, but he didn't want to spend it behind a desk. He was too old for active duty so upon the suggestion of two detectives, Dan Breece and Sterling Ford, they assigned him to the keep an eye on me.

This was supposed to make it hard for me to see Lola.

Nikki spoke up, "He's my man now!"

"Well, he has good taste," he said. "You are a very pretty girl."

From that time on, the three of us had breakfast, drank coffee and talked for hours. Cutter seemed to be lonely and looked forward to having that time with us.

Nikki's day job was working in a beauty parlor, so when she had an early appointment, Cutter would follow me when I took her home, park right behind me and fall asleep. When I was ready to leave, I would go wake him up and tell him I was going home now and that he should too and get some sleep.

He would say, "OK, Jones. I'll see you tomorrow."

We would both go our separate ways.

About four months into his following us, I noticed he was there less and less. Sometimes there would be two or three days that he was nowhere to be found. Nikki would say, "I wonder where Mr. Cutter is?" Can you imagine that we actually missed the guy??

In Kansas City, the liquor stores closed at 1:30 a.m. Sunday morning and didn't open again until 6a.m. Monday morning. This made Sunday all day and night prime time to sell bootleg whiskey. I also sold ice cold beer and bowls of chili. So Nikki and I had a full house all weekends. We did very, very well.

I soon had the money to put a down payment on a brand new Mercury, but I had no credit, so I got my mom to co-sign. She agreed on one condition; that I would get a job at the Chevrolet factory in Leeds. She had a long time friend who worked there for twenty years to use his influence to get me the job. I was anxious to get my car so I agreed. I filled out the application and returned it.

I asked for the man whom I had been told to see and an interview was arranged that following Friday. I was hired and told to report to work that following Monday. I worked a full week and got my car that weekend. My shift was from 5 p.m. to 1:30 a.m. at my mother's request. Why??? That was when all the clubs closed.

After work on Friday nights, I would pick Nikki up and take her to breakfast. I had been working for about one month and a half. While Nikki and I were having breakfast, Jack Cutter walked in. We were really happy to see him. He was dressed in civilian clothes and wore a big smile on his face. He looked about ten years younger and actually looked very happy not be a cop anymore. He said he had driven by a few times and hadn't seen my car so he didn't stop.

I explained that I had a new car now and how my mom helped me get a job at the Chevrolet plant and she helped me get a new car so I would get there.

"What a wonderful mother you have," he commented. "She stayed and prayed through all you put her through."

I totally agreed with him and the next two months things were good.

chapter five

More Trouble

Suddenly, here comes more trouble. A co-worker, who rode to and from work with me, asked me to take him to a restaurant after work one Friday night to get some chicken. I waited in the car while he went to order his food. When the waitress came to take his order, he began to flirt with her. She rejected his advances and told him to give up. As she was writing the order, he placed his hand on hers, not realizing the big man sitting next to him was her husband. The man violently pushed him to the floor and yelled to keep his hands off of his wife. My friend was wrong and instead of being apologetic, he became angry and wanted to fight. The owners made them go to the parking lot.

I heard the noise and saw the people gathering, so I got out of my car to get a closer look. I saw it was my friend under this huge monster of a man being beaten mercilessly and he was a bloody mess. Although I wanted no part of this big man, I grabbed the man's arm from behind and yelled, "You're killing him" twice.

When the man grabbed me with both hands, my friend managed to get from under him and on to his feet and run away.

The man dragged me in the restaurant and they told him the police were on the way. When they got there everybody was trying to talk at the same time and while they weren't looking, I decided to slip out the back door. To my surprise, my car was still there running and I took off to go home. As I was leaving, I saw my friend on his hands and knees crawling. I picked him up and took him home with me. I discovered why he didn't see me; his eye was swollen shut and beaten to a deep purple.

When we arrived at work on Monday, we were both handcuffed and arrested. During the fight, the big brute had beaten my friend's hat with his badge on it, off his head.

Since he was on parole from Michigan, he had violated his parole. He begged me to help him leave town; he didn't' want to go back to prison in Jackson. I felt so sorry for him he was already beaten to a pulp, so I agreed to drive him to Los Angeles.

When I told my mother, she began to cry uncontrollably saying, "Please, baby, don't do that. Look at all the trouble it has caused you trying to help your friend. Will you ever learn?"

I told my mom that I loved her to no end, but that is the way I am; I can't help it. Every friend whom I tried to help was someone that I grew up with in Leeds from kindergarten on. Their parents are friends of yours from grade school on. We were all underprivileged from Leeds and we formed a bond to always help each other. I told my mother that when she prayed for me, to make sure to thank God for letting me be the one that didn't need help and giving me the strength to help my friends.

She stopped crying, and said, "Since you put it like that, it doesn't hurt so

much". She then added, "Just be careful and keep in touch with me."

So off we went on our way. California was over 1700 mile drive and we made it in record time.

In Kansas City, when you buy a new car, the license plates are mailed to you and mine hadn't gotten there yet. I had no plates on the car, but I had the bill of sale in the glove box. In Kansas City that is all I needed, not so in Los Angeles. We got pulled over by the LAPD and they were so sure the car was stolen, we were charged with Grand Theft Auto and the car was towed. I tried to tell them I had the bill of sale, but they paid me no attention. They finally got around to checking and found out that my friend was wanted in Michigan. They came and got him and took him back to Michigan. The police told me where my car was and told me I had 48 hours to leave Los Angeles. If I ever came back, I would have to work a legitimate job for at least a year before I could be considered a resident. I told him to tell me how to get my car back

and he could have forty of those hours back! Just give me the eight.

I got my car, filled it up and hit Route 66. I returned to Kansas City in record time. When I got to my mother's house and knocked on the door, my youngest sister answered the door. I noticed a man sitting on the couch. My sister introduced him as her boyfriend, Joe. He said he met her at a bar I used to hang out at and I began to tell him of my trip to Los Angeles.

All of a sudden, there was a big boom and the next thing I knew, the door was lying on the floor. Like a nightmare from the past, there stood Dan Breece and Sterling Ford. They stood there with their guns cocked and aimed at me. They asked to see Joe's ID, and told him to be careful with whom he associated.

Meantime, I had no idea what all this was about. They told me I was under arrest for first degree murder and arrested my sisters as well for harboring a criminal. Talk about being in the dark. I had been back for less than an hour and was back in jail for murder AGAIN!

How unreal was this?? I asked some of the police, "Who got killed?"

They just ignored me. But things began to come to light on the next morning when the morning paper came out.

It seems someone went up to a meat market on 31st and Brooklyn and tried to rob a man. For some reason, the robber shot the man three times and ran from the store. As he ran, his hat came off, and an eyewitness got a pretty good look at him. The description was short, curly hair and brown-skinned. When my old enemy detectives, Breece and Ford, heard the description, they wanted it to be me. Their hatred for my seeing Lola blinded them from doing some intelligent investigation or they would have found out that I had been out of town.

I must have been entering the city just as the attempted robbery was taking place. By questioning my sister, they found out that Joe, her boyfriend, had his hair processed and curled. Also, he had shot another man on 27th and Prospect with the same caliber weapon, and although the man never pressed charges, he told them who shot him. This happened when I was locked up in

L.A. for car theft. They sent both bullets to ballistics. They discovered that both bullets came from the same gun. The Police knew then without a doubt that it couldn't have been me. They also realized that the man those two idiots, Breece and Ford, told to get out of my Mom's house was really the murderer.

All the publicity that headlined the newspapers and news on T.V., was based on Breece and Ford's report, so when I went to my preliminary hearing the charges were dismissed against me. This made those two racist bastards look like the stupid fools they were. When my mother and I walked out of court, there stood Breece and Ford. They came up to me and said, "These courts keep letting you go. We are going to catch you on a dark street one night and blow your fuckin' head off."

"If you two dirty motherfuckers are on a dark street I'll see your white asses first and we will see who gets shot," I retorted.

Mother shouted, "Brother, be quiet, don't say that!"

But it was too late. They grabbed me and slammed me face first against the

REBEL WITH A CAUSE

wall, handcuffed me and took me across the street to the city jail. What happened after that was beyond belief; the way I was treated was more criminal than anything I had ever done. They beat me up for two days, charged me with assault and took me back to the county jail. The first unbelievable thing was that there was no victim. The Kansas City Police Dept. was the complaining witnesses! Did I assault the whole damn department? By law, you were supposed to be taken to arraignment for bond to be set; it never happened. It's illegal to deprive you of the opportunity to be arraigned.

My mother and I tried everything we knew to bring attention to this and the illegal way they were keeping me locked up. Seven months passed and my mother had somehow managed to save five hundred dollars. Someone referred her to an attorney, called, "The Ghost."

His name was Richard Kerwin and he promised my mother that for five hundred dollars he could have me plea to a lesser charge. The charge would be common assault. Since I had been in jail for seven months, he could get time served. He convinced my mom and she convinced me.

Two weeks later, we went to court expecting to be set free and were shocked back to reality. The judge asked me did I wish to plead guilty to common assault and I said yes. He then sentenced me to the maximum sentence that the charge carried and that was one year in the county jail; we had been tricked.

Mr. Kerwin spoke up. "Your Honor, Mr. Jones has already been incarcerated for seven month and we were hoping you would give him time served."

The judge turned red and snatched his glasses off. "Mr. Kerwin," he said, "I should give you a year for asking for good time for this man. Not only will I not give him time served, but he is to serve everyday of the twelve months. Have you seen what this man has been doing?"

I knew then he was referring to Lola. Usually a year could be served in nine months; however, they were trying to make an example of me to discourage other blacks from dating white girls and Breece and Ford were leading the way.

They didn't care how many laws they broke to succeed. I often wonder how they could get away with this since it was all on record and who keeps better records than the police. I thought to myself that one day I will expose these bastards. In the meantime, I had to remember what Grandpa taught me and deal with whatever the next twelve months bring.

chapter six

The county jail consisted of four tanks for blacks, F-G-H and I, and all were located on the 13th floor. Tanks for the women and the whites were on the 12th floor. Each tank had six eight-men cells and a bullpen. Each tank had a key man who was allowed to have double rations of food and was the only one that could change the T.V. channel; in short, he was the boss of the tank.

Relatives could put money on the books for you to purchase goods from the commissary, which came to the tank every day. The commissary sold things like cigarettes, candy, toothpaste, cookies, stamped envelopes, etc. Each time a new inmate

was assigned to a tank, he was given a mattress, a mattress cover, a pillow and a blanket.

The jailer took me to "I" tank, unlocked the door and yelled, "Key man, new man." In the center of the bullpen was an iron table made like a picnic table. Sitting in the middle of the table with his feet on each side, a big funky looking dude told me to put my stuff down. He introduced himself as the key man, Teddy Gooch. "Are you hungry?" he asked.

"Starving!" I admitted.

They don't feed you in the city jail.

Gooch yelled to a guy named Gangsta, whom he introduced as his assistant, to bring me a sandwich. The sandwich consisted of stale lunch meat between two pieces of stale bread, but it didn't matter. I was for real hungry.

I finished it so fast, Gooch commented, "Damn, Blood, you really are hungry. Do you want another one?"

"Yes," I said, "I could use another one and he called to Gangsta and I was given another sandwich along with a few cookies. When I heard that I remembered some of the things I heard about assholes who gave people things for the purpose of demanding sex.

As I was eating the rest of the food, I was planning an attack on Gooch's big ass. One of his front teeth were missing so I figured that was a good place to start. Sure enough, when I had finished eating, he told Gangsta to put my mattress in his cell and declared I would be sleeping with him tonight.

Before Gangsta could get there, I hit Gooch with one of those lean back right hands that bloodied his face and knocked him off the table. Once on the floor, I tapdanced on his big ass until he was waving his hands, crying, "I am sorry, Blood, I'm sorry!"

I kicked him in the mouth one more time and kicked out his other big tooth next to that gap.

Gangsta came out and convinced me to let him call the jailer so they could get him to the hospital. He wasn't worth getting a murder case for. They drug his bloody ass out and I announced I was the new keyman and if anyone had any other ideas come out to the bullpen and we could settle it right now. There were no takers and I told Gangsta he could

be my assistant keyman and he said no problem.

Gangsta said that ordinarily at 6:00 a.m. each morning the mop, the mop ringer and the bucket were brought to the tank for the toilet area and shower to be cleaned. Each tank had a mop man selected by the assistant key man.

The jailer whose name was JayBird put the mop bucket in the floor so someone could clean up Gooch's blood. JayBird wanted to know who did so much damage to Gooch. Gangsta told him it was the new man.

"How in the world did such a little guy do that much damage to Gooch?" JayBird asked.

Gangsta said the first punch put Gooch out of commission and it was all downhill after that.

There were four more incidents that led to my sending inmates to general hospital. Each one of those incidents was handled with the mop ringer. Ten p.m. was called rack time; that's when you go back to your cell from being in the bullpen and the jailer slides the bars across the entrance of the cells. They aren't opened again until 6:00 a.m., and the jailer yells, "Keyman! Mop! Bucket!"

When there is someone who had to be put in his place, I was up early, dressed and waiting for the mop ringer. The cells were open and most of the inmates were still asleep. I would go in the cell of the intended victim and hit him real hard on the leg or foot. This made them spring up, hitting their head on the bottom of the top bunk. While he was still disoriented, I'd bop him on the side of his head. Most of the time, that was enough for them to go to the hospital.

The mop ringer is an iron contraption that fits on the bucket with a handle on it. It is used to squeeze the water from the mop, so you have to carefully beat somebody's ass with it or you will wind up with a murder case.

I was only five feet seven inches tall and weighed one hundred forty pounds. My grandpa had taught me not to fight fair, first! When the people I sent to the hospital were released they were sent to another tank. There were three inmates in my tank who had been sentenced to long term at the Jefferson City, Missouri

Penitentiary and they were feverishly trying to escape before the chain pulled. (The term for the bus to the Pen.)

They begged me to help them. I was about five months short and did not want to jeopardize my release. At any rate, I had been there so long and dealt with shitheads so well that all the inmates in all four tanks had developed an enormous respect for me.

After being reminded of how chicken shit they did me to make me do all this time, I gave in and agreed to help. The Jackson County Jail was supposed to be escape proof. There had been twenty failed attempts. Three guys were going and me and Gangsta had to secretly do the planning. There were forty others there that could not know about this. Anyone of them would snitch for a bag of cookies.

We were on the thirteenth floor and for this to be a success, the entire jail had to be taken over one floor at a time. From the eleventh to the thirteenth floor there was only one jailer for each floor, and the twelfth floor had a female jailer to boot. None of them carried guns while on duty. She would be easy to overpower.

All you would have to do was put her in the tank and lock the door so she could not get to a phone.

After her keys were taken, the eleventh floor would be the most difficult because that was where everyone was brought in. The jailer was there behind a bullet proof window and the elevators were about ten feet from the glass. But since we planned this for a Sunday morning, there was a good chance the door that locked them behind the counter would be open since there was no one brought in on Sunday.

There were two sets of elevators; one went from the eleventh floor to the upper floors where the inmates were housed. The others went from the eleventh floor down to the street level.

The break would start from my tank when JayBird opened the tank to put the mop bucket in. I told them to be dressed and ready to go and to remember not to hurt JayBird. Just take his handcuffs off and handcuff him to the pipe in the ceiling, take his keys and close and lock the door.

Remember what to do on the twelfth floor and once that was done, stop and relax your brain for a few minutes.

Carefully go to the eleventh floor, and you could see from the elevator door, if the side door to the cage was open. If it was, take the deputy to a closet, handcuff him to something close the door and take the elevator down to the ground floor. Walk casually out and find a cab, go to this address in Leeds and tell them I sent you. They would wait until after dark to drive you outside the city limits. You would be on your own from there.

When the fools left my tank that Sunday morning, they went to the other black tanks, unlocked them, went inside and asked the inmates who wanted to go home.

So now there were seven because they picked up four other long timers from the other tanks. There were no problems with the twelfth floor and so on to the difficult floor, the eleventh floor. They got past that with no problem and now all seven were out and no one knew they were out, but the damn fools didn't follow the plan. Instead of going to Leeds in the cab, they all went to their girlfriends' houses, getting clothes, throwing the jail clothes out of the window as they drove along. How stupid was that?

In no time at all, the entire police department was on their trail. It took them three or four days to round up six of them. The seventh one took another two days before they got him back into custody. His name was Crazy Joe and he was hiding in a motel.

Now I found out why they called him 'Crazy Joe.' When the police kicked in the door to the room, Joe shot at the police, hitting one of them in the hand as he ran to the bedroom. He gave up shortly after that because he'd started a gunfight with twenty police when he only had six bullets in his gun.

chapter seven

I was a few months short of my release and I feared because the break originated from my tank, it would be delayed. I had done nineteen months for nothing, so nothing would surprise me. I thought to myself, I would just deal with whatever happens. I have dealt with all the rest of the low-life tactics of the police, I will just deal with whatever comes my way.

Grandpa had once told me, "Lil Bubba, you got to be tough enough to adjust to any given environment."

Whatever was going to happen, I felt vindicated for successfully getting seven people out of their so-called escape proof jail.

Surprisingly, my release time came and I was released without a problem. I think they were glad to get rid of me.

At last a free man again, but this time I knew how precious freedom was, so I planned to stay on the down low until I made a plan. It was really hard to lay low after being locked up for almost nineteen months.

Gradually I started to move around, avoiding crap games or any other place the police might show up. But by and by, the inevitable happened. I was getting a haircut at a friend's barber shop and in walked Breece and Ford. They snatched me out of the chair, handcuffed me and arrested me for strong arm robbery. This kind of robbery is done without a gun and usually against women.

There are two reasons for this. One, women are easier to take advantage of and two, it doesn't require a weapon. This means this is done by a coward.

I made bond and figured this had to be some of Breece and Ford's shit. I was convinced even more it was them because I was arrested again for the same thing, but this time by two uniformed officers. Again I made bond and this time

I stayed off the streets for more than two weeks, but when I went to my hearing for the first charge, I was arrested again and I made bond again.

My bondsmen, Bruno, had lots of connection. He told me there were three ladies that actually got strong armed. He liked me and told me that he knew it was not my M.O. It must be somebody who resembled me in some small way. This would enable the police to accuse me of them.

"You know how much they hate you!" he said.

I said that makes sense because I had been completely puzzled as to what was going on. That bit of information helped to put my head on straight.

I, too, had a lot of connections from being in jail for eighteen months, 26 days. Every crook from every part of Kansas City had been in one of those black tanks and knew of me; most importantly, they respected me. I put word on the street that I wanted to know who was strong arming those ladies. I let it be known that I was being charged and I already had four bonds for it. My headquarters was on 31st and Prospect at my friends

all night restaurant. People who wanted to get in touch with me would go there, and if I wasn't there, they would leave a message.

Five days after I put the message out, the waitress called and said that she had a very important message. I told her I would be there in twenty minutes, but I was there in ten. The message gave me a written message from a fellow who had been in my tank for a couple of weeks. He was from the west side, and when they put him in my tank, he was scared to death. He was a shy guy who was rather meek. I befriended him and gave him a stamped envelope to write his family and tell them where he was. When they came to visit him on Saturday, I talked to his mother and brother. I sent them to my bondsman, Bruno, to assist them with getting him released. He was out by Monday afternoon and didn't forget me.

When he heard I was looking for whoever was strong-arming these ladies, he knew exactly who it was. He hung out in the same pool room with the dude. His message said that the dude's name was Jeremiah Byers and that he had a big mouth and would brag about whatever he did while he was drinking. He gave me the address to the pool room and a description of him. He had processed hair, was about my size and wore a faint mustache. He signed the message, "Your friend Felix. P.S. Please destroy this note. They would kill me if they knew who told you."

I put the note in my wallet and started to leave. As I got to the door the same two cops who arrested me before said, "Jones, we have another warrant for your arrest."

"What for?" I asked, heaving a deep sigh.

They said, "Same thing."

I took the note from my wallet and told the cops I was going to leave my bondsman's phone number with the waitress. The waitress wrote his name and number on the back of the note and I told her to call him and have him meet me at the city jail, same charge. I did that so as not to have the note in my possession when I got there.

Bruno was waiting there with the bond. I told him I knew who was doing the robberies and he reminded me that there was no bond for murder. I told him

I knew that already and I was just going to ask him to stop.

Bruno was a short fat Jewish gentleman with a protruding stomach, who always had a cigar butt in the corner of his mouth. He looked at me kind of funny. "Yeah, right."

Now I was out on four bonds and this shit had to stop. So I got up early the next morning, went back to the restaurant, picked up the address and a pistol, then headed to the West Side.

I found the pool room, went in and asked for Jeremiah. I told the man who ran the pool hall that I didn't come for trouble. I explained that Jeremiah had been strong- arm robbing people that I was getting the blame for. I also told him that I was out on four bonds already and I came here to ask him to stop. I told him that I would not tell the police, but if he didn't stop, I would personally stop him. Because I had come to his hood and left that threat, Byers got mad and made the mistake of coming to my corner to, as he put it, "Put a hurtin' on me."

I saw him outside the restaurant and thought he fit the description. I went outside and asked him if he was Jeremiah

Byers. He answered 'yes,' and at that point, I hit him very hard in the nose. He fell to the sidewalk and started to reach in his back pocket. He pulled out a gun, but didn't get a chance to use it. I kicked him in the throat and he dropped it. I picked it up, but I didn't try to shoot him. I just wanted to beat him up real bad.

As I was stomping him, I saw a car door open and four of his friends rushed towards us. I pointed the pistol at them and they put on the brakes fast, turned and ran like hell the opposite way. I then went back to work on Byers, this time hitting him with the gun. After I knocked three or four holes in his head, the police sped up with the spot light on me. They yelled at me, "Drop the gun or we will shoot."

I slid the gun towards the police. They called an ambulance for him and handcuffed me. They asked me where the gun came from and I told them the truth. They said that they had to charge me with possession of an unlawful firearm.

After all, it was in my possession while I was beating Byers in the head. That didn't bother me because at that

time the penalty in Kansas City was fifty dollars fine or ten days on a work farm.

The cops had followed the ambulance to the emergency room. After they finished stitching Byers up, treating the holes in his head, they arrested him. When he saw me, he started telling the police he wanted to prosecute me for attempted murder. So I them, "He is the son of a bitch that has been doing the strong-arm robberies that I am presently under four bonds for."

The next day I made bond on the gun charge, got a court date and went to an attorney named Costello. He agreed to defend me on the strong-arm charges, but told me not to pay the fine, but to go to work farm. He told me the ten days, would only be seven and that way they can't give you anymore cases. Within that time, he guaranteed me he would get all those cases dismissed. He said that the police was holding Byers for 72 hours, so the ladies could make a positive identification. I told him I hoped that I hadn't disfigured him too much for them to recognize him.

I went to court for the gun, and got the fifty dollar fine. Costello told the judge

I had no money, so I would take the 10 days. He assured me he would dispose of the other charges.

They worked my ass off at the farm, shoveling corn into a corn shucking machine. I was doing back breaking shit. Slowly the seven days passed, and when they gave me back my street clothes, they washed my suit, shrinking it. I thought it was a pretty good suit, but evidently it wasn't; it was cheap. I bought it from a thief on the corner. Lying bastard!!

As we sat there waiting for the van to take us back to town, I must have looked like a damn fool. My left pant leg had shrunk to just below my knee and the right one was just above my ankle. My coat was squeezing the hell out of me like a straight jacket.

To add insult to injury, the superintendent came out and told me I had a phone call in his office. As I walked back to his office, the other inmates fell out laughing at that suit. However, the call was bad news; it was from Costello telling me all but one case had been dismissed. He told me when I got back to town, they were going to book me back into the County Jail. My heart dropped.

Just the thought of going back to the county jail sent chills through my whole body.

The van finally came. They called it the "black Mariah." We loaded up and headed back to the city. When the van pulled into the basement of the city jail off Twelfth Street, two of the yearly regular people who committed crimes at the beginning of winter were there. They do this to get a certain sentence that will last until spring, giving them a warm place to stay with meals all winter.

Anyway, I looked out the back window and saw that the police had not closed the big door we came in. I grabbed the two fools and threw them back to the front of the van so I could be first to get out. The van had two doors that met right in the center of the van and to prevent people in the van from kicking the open, they put a heavy chain through both door handles. As they pulled the chain through the handle, I readied myself to hit whoever opened those doors. The cop opened both doors at the same time. With both of his hands occupied and his chin sticking up to meet my right hand. When I hit him, he fell straight back and hit his head on the concrete. I jumped out of the van and out the still opened back door. I ran right on to 18th Street until I couldn't run anymore.

I decided to walk up 18th Street to the first red light. I would wait for the first car that pulled up with the passenger door unlocked and I would just get in. I was lucky. The first car that rolled up was driven by an older white man. When I jumped in, I told him I meant him no harm—that I just needed a ride to Benton Boulevard. He didn't even look at me. He kept his head straight and his hands on the steering wheel. When we got to Benton, he pulled to the side and I got out, wishing him many many thanks.

chapter eight

I Was Warned To Get To Get Out Of Town

chapter eight

I Was Warned To Get Out Of Town

My mother lived 5-6 blocks down on Benton Boulevard, so I jogged to her house. When my mother saw me, she said, "My God, brother, what happened to your clothes?"

I started to tell her what happened and the phone began to ring. When she picked up the phone and said hello, all I could hear was a man's voice on the other end and my mother repeating, "Oh, my God!" Then she said, "Thank you, Mr. Cutter," and hung up the phone. She turned to me with tears running down her face. "Brother that was Mr. Cutter telling me to get you out of town. The police just issued a shoot on sight order. The policeman you hit is in the hospital

in critical condition with a concussion from hitting his head on the concrete. 'If they see him, they will kill him.' Mr. Cutter said."

My mother then called my sister and told her to come right over. She told her they had to get me out of town right away or I would be killed on sight. My sister was there in 10 minutes, with an arm full of her clothing. I had already changed into a pair of khaki pants and rolled up both pants legs so the coat would cover the pants legs. My sister brushed my hair down into bangs, tied a silk scarf on my head and put red lipstick on my lips. I took off my loafers, and put them in my back pockets. I then put on a pair of her high heels. She helped me in to her trench coat and about that time her boyfriend arrived.

He took us to Union Station; we stayed in the car as my mother went in and bought a train ticket to Detroit, Michigan.

The train was leaving in 45 minutes. To get to the trains, I had to walk about 100 yards. No way was I able to do that in those high heels. So my sister's boyfriend

put his arm around my waist and literally held me up as we walked. That was a long walk, but we finally made it. It took most of the forty minutes, so when we got there, it was time to board. I selected a window seat; I was so tired I fell asleep before we left the station. I figured when we pulled into Detroit there would be a police welcoming committee, so I had to figure a way to get off that damn train, before we got to Detroit.

My sister, Willetta, (we called her Lady Bug,) lived in Ypsilanti, Michigan, which was about 28 miles before you get to Detroit. I remember there was no train station there, but to my surprise the train stopped in Ann Arbor. I tried the window and it slid right up. I promptly stepped out the window and went behind a small building and took off all that woman shit. I wiped off the lipstick, threw away those damn high heels, and rolled down my pants legs. I took my cap out from the coat pocket, threw the coat away, walked two blocks, found a pay phone and called my sister. She drove the seven miles to pick me up. I lived with Willetta until I left for sunny California.

I got a job, worked for three years, bought myself a car and headed for Los Angeles, California. In my next book I will tell you what happened when I got there!

www.ingramcontent.com/pod-product-compliance
Lightning Source LLC
LaVergne TN
LVHW011408080426
835511LV00005B/441